The Reestablishment of the Navy, 1787–1801

HISTORICAL OVERVIEW
AND
SELECT BIBLIOGRAPHY

"Preparation for War to defend Commerce. The Swedish Church Southwark with the building of the Frigate *Philadelphia.*" W. Birch & Son. Courtesy of the Franklin D. Roosevelt Library, Hyde Park, N.Y.

NAVAL HISTORY BIBLIOGRAPHIES, NO. 4

The Reestablishment of the Navy, 1787–1801

HISTORICAL OVERVIEW

AND

SELECT BIBLIOGRAPHY

Michael J. Crawford
Christine F. Hughes

Naval Historical Center
Department of the Navy
Washington
1995

Secretary of the Navy's Advisory Subcommittee on Naval History
(as of 8 May 1995)

Pen and ink drawings by John Charles Roach

Library of Congress Cataloging-in-Publication Data

Crawford, Michael J., 1950–
    The Reestablishment of the Navy, 1787–1801 : historical overview and select bibliography / Michael J. Crawford, Christine F. Hughes.
       p.   cm.—(Naval bibliographies ; no. 4)
    Includes index.
    ISBN 0–945274–32–7 (alk. paper)
    1. United States—History, Naval—To 1900—Bibliography.
2. United States—History, Naval—To 1900.   3. United States. Navy—History—Bibliography.   4. United States.   Navy—History.
I. Hughes, Christine F., 1949– . II. Title. III. Series.
Z1249.N3C73   1995
[E182]
016.359′00973—dc20   95–19841
                                           CIP

∞ The paper used in this publication meets the requirements for permanence established by the American National Standard for Information Sciences "Permanence of Paper for Printed Library Materials" (ANSI Z 39.48–1984).

Contents

Foreword

The purpose of this publication is to encourage understanding and further study of events associated with the rebirth of the American Navy in the 1790s. In comprehending the significance of this milestone in our naval history, one needs to remember that the United States Navy traces its beginnings to the Continental Navy that was established in 1775 at the outset of the American Revolution. Following the winning of American independence, however, our nation elected to have no navy for a period of almost ten years.

America's founding fathers included provisions for a navy in the new federal constitution of 1789. But actual steps to create that service did not occur until the mid-1790s, when America's thriving overseas shipping and trade became targets of attacks and interference. These foreign threats, combined with the determination by many leaders to establish the United States as a major power, led President Washington and Congress to recognize the need to restore American defenses at sea.

It is possible to argue that the decision to re-create a navy in the turbulent decade of the 1790s is as significant an event as the founding of the Continental Navy in 1775. The nation's experiment in doing without a naval force in the years following the American Revolution proved to be entirely unsatisfactory. Simply put, we learned in this period that the United States faced unpredictable threats, from different sources and in several regions, that needed to be met by a navy capable of defending American interests on the high seas. As we approach the twenty-first century, that recognition still explains why our country needs to maintain a strong navy.

Michael J. Crawford, who heads the Naval Historical Center's Early History Branch, and his associate, Christine F. Hughes, deserve praise for the fine scholarship reflected in this volume. In addition, the Center deeply appreciates the contributions of several noted authorities on early American history who offered their criticisms and suggestions as this volume evolved through several drafts. Those individuals included William M. Fowler, Jr., Northeastern University; Harold D. Langley, Smithsonian Institution; Christopher McKee, Grinnell College; William J. Morgan, Naval Historical Center emeritus; and Michael A. Palmer, East Carolina University.

Despite the invaluable assistance they received, the authors alone are responsible for this volume. I join them in expressing the hope that this publication will be a valuable resource for any individual interested in the historical development of our nation and the American navy.

DEAN C. ALLARD
Director of Naval History

The Reestablishment
of the Navy,
1787–1801

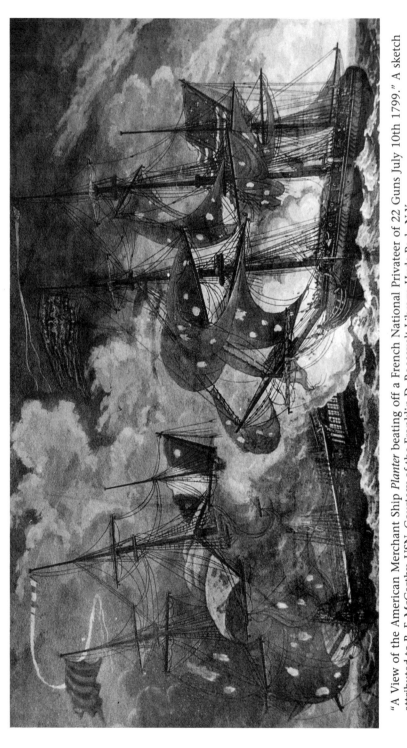

"A View of the American Merchant Ship *Planter* beating off a French National Privateer of 22 Guns July 10th 1799." A sketch attributed to B. F. McCarthy, USN. Courtesy of the Franklin D. Roosevelt Library, Hyde Park, N.Y.

Historical Overview of the Federalist Navy, 1787–1801

First Naval Legislation under the Constitution

"Without a Respectable Navy—Alas America!" wrote Captain John Paul Jones of the Continental Navy early in the American Revolutionary War.[1] After the United States won its independence, however, Congress, under the Articles of Confederation, was too weak to maintain more than a token armed force. The United States had financed the war through huge foreign loans and by issuing paper money. Without taxing power, the Confederation could not pay off the debt. Although the government possessed one tremendous asset, western lands, it would take time to transform that asset into cash. For the present, the Confederation government could not afford to maintain a single warship. The last ship of the Continental Navy, the frigate *Alliance*, was sold in 1785, and its commander, Captain John Barry, returned to civilian life. The navy disappeared and the army dwindled to a mere 700 men.

The infant Republic's military weakness further convinced American nationalists of the necessity of adopting a new constitution that would increase the authority of the national government, particularly by giving it the power of taxation. The issue of naval power, itself, produced little debate during the Constitutional Convention in 1787. The frame of government proposed by the convention gave Congress power to raise money to "provide and maintain a navy," which implies a permanent naval establishment, as contrasted with the power "to raise and support armies," which suggests that armies would exist as temporary expedients. Whereas the Constitution restricted army appropriations to two years, it left the term of naval appropriations unlimited. Navies were not thought to pose the same threat to political liberty as did standing armies. After all, as Thomas Jefferson had once observed, "a naval force can never endanger our liberties, nor occasion bloodshed; a land force would do both";[2] or, as James Madison would argue in favor of ratification of the Constitution, a navy could "never be turned by a perfidious government against our liberties."[3]

"If the new Constitution is adopted, as there is reason to expect," John Paul Jones wrote in December 1787, "America will soon be a very respectable Nation; and the creation of a Marine Force will necessarily be among the first objects of her policy."[4] Despite his wishful reasoning and the initiation of the ratified Constitution in 1789, when Jones died in 1792 the only U.S. naval force was the Treasury Department's Revenue Cutter Service, a forerunner of the United States Coast Guard.

The clear necessity of defending the nation's seaborne commerce finally moved Congress to create a navy in the spring of 1794. With the beginning of the wars of the French Revolution in 1793, British warships began interfering with American trade with France, and French warships with American trade with Great Britain. Another source of genuine danger to American commerce came from corsairs of North Africa's Barbary Coast. Raiders sailing from the ports of Morocco, Algiers, Tripoli, and Tunis had long forced European powers either to maintain naval squadrons on station in the Mediterranean or to pay annual tribute to assure non-interference with merchant shipping. Previous to the American Revolution, American merchantmen in that region enjoyed the protection of the British government, but that protection evaporated with independence. In 1785 Algerine corsairs made their first seizures of American vessels, two merchantmen, taking twenty-two passengers and crew members prisoner. Congress declined to pay ransom, and by 1793 six of the prisoners had died in captivity. In 1793 Portugal, whose navy had been keeping the Algerine corsairs within the confines of the Mediterranean, signed a truce with Algiers. Soon after, Algerines sailed into the Atlantic to prey on American merchantmen. Before the end of the year they held over 100 Americans prisoner.

Congressional debate on the wisdom of reviving the navy began in earnest at the end of 1793. In his annual address to Congress on 3 December, President Washington spoke in general terms of the nation's need to prepare to defend itself: "If we desire to avoid insult, we must be able to repel it; if we desire to secure peace . . . , it must be known, that we are at all times ready for War." [5] A few days later, news reached Philadelphia of the truce between Portugal and Algiers, opening the way for Barbary corsairs to cruise the Atlantic and imperil American trade with much of Europe. On 16 December the President forwarded to Congress documents on the unsatisfactory negotiations with the Barbary Powers. In response to these events, the House of Representatives resolved on 2 January 1794 "that a naval force adequate to the protection of the commerce of the United States, against the Algerine corsairs, ought to be provided," and appointed a committee to prepare a report on what kind of naval force would be necessary to deal with the menace. On 20 January 1794, committee chairman Thomas Fitzsimons, a Federalist from Pennsylvania, reported a resolution to authorize the procurement of six frigates, a force thought sufficient for the purpose.[6]

Despite the real threat to American commerce, congressional approval of naval legislation was far from certain. By the 1790s some theorists of republican government were arguing that navies posed greater dangers to liberty than did armies. They maintained that the major expense of constructing, fitting out, and manning warships meant large expenditures and mounting taxes, and they considered this transfer of wealth from the people via politicians into the hands of a few to be a source of political corruption. Influenced by these beliefs, several congressmen spoke in opposition to the proposal to procure six frigates. Some surmised that the Algerines were acting on behalf of the British and that going to war with the former would risk an Anglo-American war. They thought that paying tribute would be wiser and cheaper than building a navy. One congressman even suggested the alternative of hiring the Portuguese navy to protect American commerce. Opponents of the naval measure also questioned whether the six frigates proposed would be adequate to the object intended, and whether negotiation would not be a less costly and more effective means of attaining the desired end.

The pro-navy side was strengthened when the President sent documentation supporting the view that a navy was essential, and by the almost simultaneous arrival of distressing news that the British had prohibited all neutral trade with the French West Indies. The "Act to provide a naval armament," authorizing the President to acquire six frigates, four of forty-four guns each and two of thirty-six, by purchase or otherwise, passed the House of Representatives by a vote of fifty to thirty-nine. Those congressmen who voted in favor came principally from cities that depended on maritime trade, and from the northern and eastern regions. Opponents came from rural areas, the south, and the frontier. The act passed the Senate and was signed by the President on 27 March 1794.

Secretary of War Henry Knox, responsible for the construction of these ships, reported to Congress in December 1794 that the passing of the act

> created an anxious solicitude that this second commencement of a navy for the United States should be worthy of their national character. That the vessels should combine such qualities of strength, durability, swiftness of sailing, and force, as to render them equal, if not superior, to any frigates belonging to any of the European Powers.[7]

His succinct phrase, "this second commencement of a navy for the United States," summarized the resounding significance of this act. The "anxious solicitude" felt by the nation's leaders led to the design and building of superb ships of war.

Construction of the First Six Frigates

Without a Department of the Navy, implementation of the 1794 naval legislation fell to the Department of War, headed by Henry Knox until 1795, Timothy Pickering from 1795 to 1796, and James McHenry from 1796 to 1798. After consulting several persons knowledgeable about warship construction, including John Foster Williams, a captain in the Massachusetts Navy during the Revolution; John Barry, a former Continental Navy captain; Joshua Humphreys, a Philadelphia shipbuilder; and James Hackett, shipbuilder for the Continental Navy at Portsmouth, New Hampshire, Knox made recommendations to Washington on 15 April 1794, which the President accepted immediately. Rather than purchasing merchant ships and converting them into men-of-war, an option under the act, Knox recommended the construction of new frigates designed to be superior to any vessel of that class in European navies. To keep labor costs down, government employees rather than private contractors would build the ships, and construction sites would be distributed geographically in order to spread the economic benefit and win popular support. "It is just and wise to proportion . . . benefits as nearly as may be to those places or states which pay the greatest amount to its support," Knox advised. Although it might be cheaper to build the frigates successively in a single place, "a few thousand dollars in the expences will be no object compared with the satisfaction a just distribution would afford." [8]

The President approved six construction sites: Portsmouth, N.H.; Boston, Mass.; New York, N.Y.; Philadelphia, Pa.; Baltimore, Md.; and Gosport (Norfolk), Va. At each site, a civilian naval constructor was hired to direct the work. Navy captains were appointed as superintendents, one for each of the six frigates. John Barry, last officer of the Continental Navy in active service, received commission number one as the first officer in the new United States Navy.

CONSTRUCTION OF THE FIRST SIX FRIGATES

Site	Frigate	Guns	Superintendent	Naval Constructor
Portsmouth	*Congress*	36	James Sever	James Hackett
Boston	*Constitution*	44	Samuel Nicholson	George Claghorn
New York	*President*	44	Silas Talbot	Forman Cheeseman
Philadelphia	*United States*	44	John Barry	Joshua Humphreys
Baltimore	*Constellation*	36	Thomas Truxtun	David Stodder
Gosport	*Chesapeake*	36	Richard Dale	Josiah Fox

Because of the difficulty of gathering supplies and the decision to build major structural components out of live oak, which had to be harvested in southern forests, construction proceeded slowly. In March 1795 Secretary of War Timothy Pickering prepared a list of ten suggested names for the ships. It is likely that President Washington selected five of them: *Constitution, United States, President, Constellation,* and *Congress. Chesapeake*'s name was designated some time later.

The warships were still being framed when, in early 1796, word came of a negotiated peace between the United States and Algiers, at the cost of nearly one million dollars, which included payment of ransom for the American prisoners and the cost of building the 32-gun frigate *Crescent* for the Dey's fleet. The act authorizing the six frigates called for a halt in construction in the event of peace with Algiers, but President Washington urged Congress to extend authorization to complete the six frigates.

Congress approved the completion of only three of the frigates. The other three would remain in their partially constructed state. Accordingly, on 20 April 1796 the President signed the "Act supplementary to an act, entitled 'An act to provide a naval armament.'" Under the terms of the 1796 act the frigate *United States* was launched at Philadelphia on 10 May 1797; the *Constellation,* at Baltimore on 7 September 1797; and the *Constitution,* at Boston on 21 October 1797.

In his last annual address to Congress in December 1796, President Washington urged "the gradual creation of a navy" for the protection of the country's commerce.[9] Nevertheless, during the ensuing year Congress remained divided over whether to allow the three new frigates to fit out and man in preparation for duty at sea. In July 1797, however, the French government's disdain for American rights to trade with France's enemies prompted Congress to authorize the President to man and employ the three frigates.

France had been America's major ally in the War of Independence, and without its assistance the United States may not have won independence. The new government of Revolutionary France viewed a 1794 commercial agreement between the United States and Great Britain, known as Jay's Treaty, as a violation of France's 1778 treaties with the United States. The French increased their seizures of American ships trading with their British enemies and refused to receive a new United States minister when he arrived in Paris in December 1796. In his annual message to Congress at the close of 1797, President John Adams reported on France's refusal to negotiate and spoke of the need "to place our country in a suitable posture of defense."[10] In April of 1798 President Adams informed Congress of the infamous "X Y Z Affair," in which three French agents demanded a large bribe for the restoration of relations with the United States. Outraged by this affront to national honor, on 27 April 1798 Congress authorized the President to acquire, arm, and man no more than twelve vessels, of up to twenty-two guns each. Under the terms of this act several vessels were purchased and converted into ships of war. One of these, the *Ganges*, a Philadelphia-built merchant ship, became "the first man-of-war to fit out and get to sea [24 May 1798] under the second organization of the Navy."[11]

In March 1798 an overworked Secretary of War James McHenry brought before Congress the problem of his responsibility for naval affairs. Naval administration had become a significant portion of his department's work, as it had for the Department of the Treasury, which oversaw all the navy's contracting and disbursing. The Department of War also had received congressional criticism for what was seen as the mismanagement and the excessive cost of the naval construction program. In addition, the growing trouble with the French induced Congress to authorize an increase in the size of the navy and raised the possibility that the navy would be called on to confront French privateers.

In response to the obvious need for an executive department responsible solely for, and staffed with persons competent in, naval affairs, Congress passed a bill establishing the Department of the Navy. President John Adams signed that historic act on 30 April 1798. Benjamin Stoddert, a Maryland merchant who served as secretary to the Continental Board of War during the American Revolution, became the first secretary of the navy. One historian writes that Stoddert "was a classic Navalist" who "desired an American navy which could, not only protect commerce, but which would increase American prestige."[12]

On 28 May Congress authorized the public vessels of the United States to capture armed French vessels hovering off the coast of the United States, initiating the undeclared Quasi-War with France. That conflict led to the rapid passage of several pieces of naval legislation. An act of 30 June gave the President authority to accept ships on loan from private citizens, who would be paid in interest-bearing government bonds. On 9 July Congress authorized U.S. naval vessels to capture armed French vessels anywhere on the high seas, not just off the coast of the United States. This act also sanctioned the issuance of privateering commissions. Two days later, the President signed the act that established the United States Marine Corps. On 16 July Congress appropriated funds to build and equip the three remaining frigates begun under the Act of 1794: *Congress,* launched at Portsmouth, N.H., on 15 August 1799; *Chesapeake,* at Gosport, Va., on 2 December 1799; and *President,* at New York, N.Y., on 10 April 1800.

Quasi-War with France

Secretary of the Navy Stoddert realized that the navy possessed too few warships to protect a far-flung merchant marine by using convoys or by patrolling the North American coast. Rather, he concluded that the best way to defeat the French campaign against American shipping was by offensive operations in the Caribbean, where most of the French cruisers were based. Thus at the very outset of the conflict, the Department of the Navy adopted a policy of going to the source of the enemy's strength. Nevertheless, by 1799, in response to the merchants' insistent demands for protection, naval vessels were convoying merchant ships in the Caribbean in addition to cruising against the enemy.

When Stoddert became secretary in June 1798, only one American naval vessel was deployed. By the end of the year a force of twenty ships was planned for the Caribbean. Before the war ended, the force available to the navy approached thirty vessels, with some 700 officers and 5,000 seamen.

The highlight of the first year of the undeclared war was the capture by Thomas Truxtun's *Constellation* of the French frigate l'*Insurgente* in February 1799. In addition, American naval vessels seized nineteen French privateers during the winter of 1798–99. The French challenge to American naval forces increased late in 1799 as six French warships arrived in the Antilles with instructions to intensify the commercial war. The American squadrons responded aggressively. *Constellation* fought to a draw the more powerful la *Vengeance* on 1 February 1800. Silas Talbot engineered an expedition in the Puerto Plata harbor in St. Domingo, a possession of France's ally Spain, on 11 May 1800 in which a naval force under Lieutenant Isaac Hull cut out the French privateer *Sandwich* from the harbor and spiked the guns in the Spanish fort. By the end of the war American ships had made prizes of approximately eighty-five French vessels. American successes resulted from a combination of Stoddert's administrative skill in deploying effectively his limited forces and the initiative of his seagoing officers.

Although they were fighting the same enemy, the Royal Navy and the United States Navy did not cooperate operationally, nor did they share operational plans or come to mutual understandings about deployment of their forces. The British did sell the American government naval stores and munitions. And the two navies shared a system of signals by which to recognize each other's warships at sea and allowed merchantmen of their respective nations to join their convoys.[13]

By October 1800, the aggressiveness of the cruisers of the United States Navy, as well as of those of the Royal Navy, combined with a more conciliatory diplomatic stance by the French toward America, produced a reduction in the activity of the French privateers and warships. In mid-December 1800 news reached Washington that a peace treaty with France (Convention of Mortefontaine, 30 September 1800) ended the Quasi-War.

The war highlighted several weaknesses in the fledgling navy, both in the shore establishment and in the operational forces. Problems arose in procurement, provisioning, manning of ships, delegation of authority, and planning for an extensive campaign. Squadron commanders learned that they required smaller ships to pursue enemy privateers in shallow waters. Many of the merchantmen converted into men-of-war proved to be poor sailers. During the first year of the war, Stoddert did not fully coordinate the rotation of vessels refitting in port with those on stations requiring relief. By restricting the enlistments in the navy to one year, Congress effectively limited the time that ships could remain deployed. The leadership qualities among Stoddert's senior officers varied widely and politics and personal jealousies often stymied his attempts to assign them to the navy's best advantage. One of the navy's senior officers, Captain Isaac Phillips, was dismissed for permitting a British officer to board his ship, USS *Baltimore,* and press several seamen.

Despite these problems, the newly reestablished United States Navy acquitted itself well during the Quasi-War and succeeded in achieving its limited goal of stopping the depredations of the French ships against American commerce. In the war, the navy proved itself an effective instrument of national policy.

Federalist Legacy

Secretary of the Navy Stoddert was concerned not only with daily administrative and operational activities but also with increasing the navy's strength for the future. Using some of the money Congress appropriated for shipbuilding, Stoddert established six navy yards. In a December 1798 proposal to Congress, he also advocated building twelve ships of the line, twelve frigates, and twenty ships of up to twenty-four guns. Congress initially approved the construction of six ships of the line. But as the war with France wound down in 1800 the prospects for a stronger naval force dimmed. President John Adams shared Stoddert's commitment to a strong navy. Whereas Adams supported a cruiser navy, however, his secretary wanted to build ships of the line, keep thirteen frigates, and sell off the smaller vessels. Stoddert reasoned that in the event of another war the government could purchase smaller vessels more readily than larger ones. The navy needed to have the larger vessels built before any conflict erupted because of their lengthy construction process. Congress, in a cost-cutting mood, adopted the Peace Establishment Act, which kept the frigates but eliminated construction of the ships of the line and drastically reduced the officer corps. Adams could have left this naval legislation to the new Jeffersonian Republican administration, which won the fall 1800 elections, but reasoned that the Jeffersonians might make even deeper cuts. In one of his last duties as President, he signed the act on 3 March 1801.

President Thomas Jefferson commenced his administration intent on reducing the navy's budget. Renewed problems with the Barbary States in 1801, however, forced him to send a small squadron to the Mediterranean as a show of force. Before the American squadron could leave its native shores, Tripoli declared war on the United States, compelling the President to wage a prolonged overseas war that did not conclude until 1805. In effect, therefore, this conflict resulted in the Republicans confirming their political opponents' fateful decision in the 1790s to reestablish a United States Navy.

During the first dozen years under the Constitution, the new nation grappled with the difficulties of developing a naval force. In giving the navy its "second commencement," the nation's executive and legislative leaders dealt with problems relating to finance, warship technology and design, an infrastructure of shipyards and shipwrights, sources of raw materials and naval stores, necessary force size, officering, and manning. They struggled with these challenges within the contexts of a complex international situation and of concerns about constitutional authority, high taxes, cost overruns, and political corruption. Ultimately, the United States Navy was reestablished with the purposes of defending the country's commerce and asserting its rights on the high seas as a sovereign nation.

Notes

1. John Paul Jones to Robert Morris, 17 Oct. 1776, *Naval Documents of the American Revolution,* edited by William Bell Clark et al., 9 vols. to date (Washington: Naval Historical Center, 1964–), 6:1303.

2. Thomas Jefferson to James Monroe, 11 Aug. 1786, in *The Papers of Thomas Jefferson,* edited by Julian P. Boyd et al., 25 vols. to date (Princeton, N.J.: Princeton University Press, 1950–), 10:225.

3. "The Federalist Number 41," in *The Papers of James Madison,* edited by William T. Hutchinson et al., 17 vols. to date (Chicago: University of Chicago Press, 1962–), 10:395.

4. John Paul Jones to François-Louis Teissèdre de Fleury, ca. Dec. 1787, Smithsonian Institution, Washington, D.C.

5. George Washington, "Fifth Annual Address to Congress," 3 Dec. 1793, in *The Writings of George Washington from the Original Manuscript Sources, 1745–1799,* edited by John C. Fitzpatrick, 39 vols. (Washington: Government Printing Office, 1931–1944), 33:166.

6. United States Congress, *American State Papers. Documents, Legislative and Executive, of the Congress of the United States,* 38 vols. (Washington: Gales and Seaton, 1832–1861), Class VI, Naval Affairs, 1:5.

7. Ibid., 6.

8. Henry Knox to George Washington, 15 April 1794, George Washington Papers, Library of Congress, Washington, D.C.

9. George Washington, "Eighth Annual Address," 7 Dec. 1796, in *A Compilation of the Messages and Papers of the Presidents, 1789–1897,* compiled by James D. Richardson, 10 vols. (Washington: Government Printing Office, 1896–1899), 1:201.

10. John Adams, "First Annual Address," 22 Nov. 1797, in ibid., 251.

11. United States Naval History Division, *Dictionary of American Naval Fighting Ships,* edited by James L. Mooney et al., 8 vols. (Washington: Government Printing Office, 1959–1981), 3:17, s.v. *Ganges.*

12. Craig L. Symonds, *Navalists and Antinavalists: The Naval Policy Debate in the United States, 1785–1827* (Newark, Del.: University of Delaware Press, 1980), 72.

13. Michael A. Palmer, "Anglo-American Naval Cooperation, 1798–1801," *Naval History* 4 (Summer 1990): 14–20.

Needs and Opportunities for Research and Writing

The contents of this bibliography highlight the strengths and weaknesses of the scholarship on the navy of the Federalist era. Scholars have written extensively on the politics of the reestablishment of the navy; on leading policy makers, including presidents, cabinet members and congressmen; on naval officers; on early shipbuilding; and on the operations of the Quasi-War. No doubt, there is still room for future scholars to find new things to say about each of these subjects. On the naval shipbuilding program, for instance, over the course of this century scholars have debated the relative roles of Josiah Fox and Joshua Humphreys as designers of the 1790s frigates, and writers have explored several technical aspects of naval ship design. Yet, we lack a full-length biography of Humphreys and a study of naval shipbuilding as an industry during the Federalist era. Both would be valuable and original contributions.

Several other significant aspects of naval history in the Federalist era remain neglected. Almost untouched as a subject of scholarship is the economic influence of the reestablishment of the navy on the nation as well as on specific regions and towns. What impact did naval shipbuilding and the navy's demand for supplies, ordnance, and munitions, as well as sailors, have on the economy? The composition of the enlisted force and related questions—recruitment, discipline, provisioning, and living conditions—need to be studied. Topics in naval medicine want their historians. Relations between the American and British naval forces during the Quasi-War, the European reaction to the reestablishment of the American navy, and the navy's relations with civil authorities during the Quasi-War deserve further investigation. How the new federal courts applied international, admiralty, and prize law in cases involving the navy, as well as how naval personnel understood those forms of law, are worthy topics. The records of the courts, civil and military, are rich but underused sources of information about the early navy. It is generally agreed that the navy during the War of 1812 played a significant role in strengthening American nationalist sentiment, but did the navy have a similar function in the Federalist period? Studies of naval iconography in popular culture, including broadsides, ballads, prints, decorative motifs on furniture and architecture, parades, and the toasts offered at naval banquets might provide answers.

"A View of the American Frigate, *Constellation*, capturing the French National Frigate, l'*Insurgente*, within sight of Basseterre, Feb.ʸ 9th, 1799." Courtesy of the Franklin D. Roosevelt Library, Hyde Park, N.Y.

Bicentennial Award Competition

To mark the bicentennial of USS *Constitution*, which was authorized in 1794, launched in 1797, and ordered on its first cruise in 1798, as well as the bicentennial of the establishment of the Department of the Navy (1798), the Naval Historical Center will make an award of $750 for an article and an award of $2,500 for a book, related to a bicentennial theme and based on original research, published or accepted for publication between 1994 and 1998. Articles and books whose subject relates to any aspect of the history of USS *Constitution* in any time period, or to any aspect of the history of the Federal navy, ca. 1787 to 1801, are eligible.

Nominations should be made by 30 June 1998, and must include one copy of the article or book, or, if the work is not yet in print, of the manuscript along with evidence that the work has been accepted for publication. Announcement of the awards will be made in December 1998. Nominations should be sent to:

Senior Historian
Naval Historical Center
Washington Navy Yard
901 M Street SE
Washington, DC 20374–5060

An EEO/AA Employer

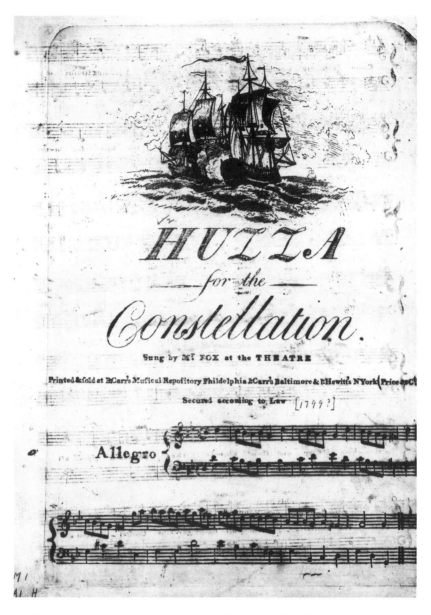

"Huzza for the *Constellation*. Sung by Mr. Fox at the Theatre." Printed at B. Carr's Musical Repository. Philadelphia, circa 1799. Naval Historical Center, Washington, D.C.

Select Bibliography of Published Works

This bibliography on the United States Navy in the Federalist period (1787–1801) represents a compilation of citations to published contemporary source materials, twentieth-century studies, and selected nineteenth-century works of particular research value. Organized topically, the entries are annotated only to explain the contents of works whose titles are not self-explanatory. *United States Naval History: A Bibliography* (Seventh Edition, 1993), published by the Naval Historical Center, lists additional general studies that may include discussion of the Federalist period.

General Studies and Monographs

1. Fowler, William M., Jr. *Jack Tars and Commodores: The American Navy, 1783–1815*. Boston: Houghton Mifflin, 1984. 318 pp.

2. Long, David F. *Gold Braid and Foreign Relations: Diplomatic Activities of U.S. Naval Officers, 1798–1883*. Annapolis: Naval Institute Press, 1988. 502 pp.

3. Nash, Howard P., Jr. *The Forgotten Wars: The Role of the U.S. Navy in the Quasi War with France and the Barbary Wars, 1798–1805*. New York: A. S. Barnes, 1968. 308 pp.

Politics, Policies, and Establishment of the Navy

4. Albion, Robert G. *Makers of Naval Policy, 1798–1947*. Edited by Rowena Reed. Annapolis: Naval Institute Press, 1980. 737 pp.

5. Anderson, William G. "John Adams and the Creation of the American Navy." Ph.D. diss., State University of New York at Stony Brook, 1975. 192 pp.

6. ———. "John Adams, the Navy, and the Quasi-War with France." *American Neptune* 30 (April 1970): 117–32.

7. Bolander, L. H. "An Incident in the Founding of the American Navy." United States Naval Institute *Proceedings* 55 (June 1929): 491–94.

A caucus in January 1794 at which several senators and representatives and Secretaries Hamilton and Knox discussed a plan for establishing a national navy.

8. Calkins, Carlos Gilman. "The American Navy and the Opinions of One of Its Founders, John Adams, 1735–1826." United States Naval Institute *Proceedings* 37 (June 1911): 453–83.

9. Carter, Edward C., II. "Mathew Carey, Advocate of American Naval Power, 1785–1814." *American Neptune* 26 (July 1966): 177–88.

A Philadelphia publisher who supported the Naval Act of 1794.

10. Frost, Holloway H. "How We Got Our Navy." United States Naval Institute *Proceedings* 59 (January 1933): 43–48.

11. Hayes, Frederic H. "John Adams and American Sea Power." *American Neptune* 25 (January 1965): 35–45.

12. Henrich, Joseph G. "The Triumph of Ideology: The Jeffersonians and the Navy, 1779–1807." Ph.D. diss., Duke University, 1971. 420 pp.

13. Kelly, John Joseph, Jr. "The Struggle for American Seaborne Independence as Viewed by John Adams." Ph.D. diss., University of Maine, 1973. 396 pp.

14. O'Connor, Raymond G. *Origins of the American Navy: Sea Power in the Colonies and New Nation*. Lanham, Md.: University Press of America, 1994. 125 pp.

15. Rogers, George C. *Evolution of a Federalist: William Loughton Smith of Charleston (1758–1812)*. Columbia: University of South Carolina Press, 1962. 439 pp.

Smith served in Congress from the First Congress until 10 July 1797 when he resigned to become minister to Portugal. He advocated a strong American naval force in the Mediterranean to keep the Barbary powers in check.

16. Rohr, John A. "Constitutional Foundations of the United States Navy: Text and Context." *Naval War College Review* 45 (Winter 1992): 68–84.

The debate between Federalists and Anti-Federalists over the constitutional basis of a navy.

17. Sharrer, G. Terry. "The Search for a Naval Policy, 1783–1812." In *In Peace and War: Interpretations of American Naval History, 1775–1984,* 2d ed., edited by Kenneth J. Hagan, 27–45. Westport, Conn.: Greenwood, 1984.

18. Smelser, Marshall. *The Congress Founds the Navy, 1787–1798.* Notre Dame, Ind.: University of Notre Dame Press, 1959. 229 pp.

19. Sofaer, Abraham D. "John Adams and Undeclared War as National Policy." In *War, Foreign Affairs and Constitutional Power: The Origins,* 131–61. Cambridge, Mass.: Ballinger, 1976.

20. Sprout, Harold, and Margaret Sprout. *The Rise of American Naval Power, 1776–1918.* 1939. Reprint. Annapolis: Naval Institute Press, 1990. 448 pp.

21. Symonds, Craig L. *Navalists and Antinavalists: The Naval Policy Debate in the United States, 1785–1827.* Newark: University of Delaware Press, 1980. 252 pp.

Naval Administration

Documents

22. Bauer, K. Jack, ed. *The New American State Papers: Naval Affairs.* 10 vols. Wilmington, Del.: Scholarly Resources, 1981.

Material selected from the Gales and Seaton *American State Papers,* the congressional serial set, and previously unpublished documents from the National Archives.

23. Stoddert, Benjamin. "Benjamin Stoddert Calls for Massive Naval Expansion." In *American Military Thought*, edited by Walter Millis, 74–78. Indianapolis: Bobbs-Merrill, 1966.

24. ———. "Letters of Benjamin Stoddert, First Secretary of the Navy, to Nicholas Johnson of Newburyport, 1798–1799." *Essex Institute Historical Collections* 74 (1938): 350–60.

25. United States Congress. *American State Papers. Documents, Legislative and Executive, of the Congress of the United States*. 38 vols. Washington: Gales and Seaton, 1832–1861. Class VI, Naval Affairs, vol. 1: March 3, 1789–March 5, 1825.

Secondary Literature

26. Albion, Robert G. "The First Days of the Navy Department." *Military Affairs* 22 (Spring 1948): 1–11.

   How Benjamin Stoddert shaped the Navy Department.

27. Carrigg, John Joseph. "Benjamin Stoddert and the Foundation of the American Navy." Ph.D. diss., Georgetown University, 1953. 367 pp.

28. ———. "Benjamin Stoddert, 18 June 1798–31 March 1801." In *American Secretaries of the Navy*, edited by Paolo E. Coletta, 1: 59–75. Annapolis: Naval Institute Press, 1980.

29. Crackel, Theodore J. "The Common Defence: The Department of War, 1789–1794." *Prologue* 21 (Winter 1989): 331–43.

30. Ford, Henry J. "Timothy Pickering." In *The American Secretaries of State and Their Diplomacy*, edited by Samuel Flagg Bemis, 2:163–244. 1928. Reprint. New York: Pageant Book, 1958.

31. Jones, Robert F. "The Naval Thought and Policy of Benjamin Stoddert, First Secretary of the Navy, 1798–1801." *American Neptune* 24 (January 1964): 61–69.

32. Paullin, Charles O. *Paullin's History of Naval Administration, 1775–1911*. Annapolis: Naval Institute Press, 1968. 485 pp.

   A collection of articles from the United States Naval Institute *Proceedings*.

33. ———. "Washington City and the Old Navy." *Records of the Columbia Historical Society* 33–34 (1932): 163–77.

34. Scheina, Robert L. "Benjamin Stoddert, Politics, and the Navy." *American Neptune* 36 (January 1976): 54–68.

35. Steiner, Bernard C. *The Life and Correspondence of James McHenry.* Cleveland: Burrows, 1907. 640 pp.

36. Turner, Harriot Stoddert. "Memoirs of Benjamin Stoddert, First Secretary of the United States Navy." *Records of the Columbia Historical Society* 20 (1917): 141–66.

   Contains Stoddert correspondence.

37. Ward, Harry M. *The Department of War, 1781–1795.* Pittsburgh: University of Pittsburgh Press, 1962. 287 pp.

38. White, Leonard D. *The Federalists: A Study in Administrative History.* New York: Macmillan, 1948. 538 pp.

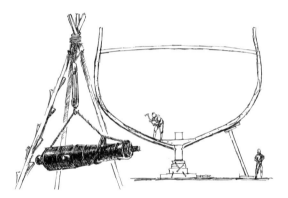

Shipbuilding and Ordnance

Documents

39. Brewington, Marion V. "Who Built the *Enterprize?*" *American Neptune* 4 (July 1944): 233–35.

   Transcription of a list of vouchers for this schooner's expenditures from 20 November 1798 to 31 January 1800.

40. "Letters from the Joshua Humphreys Collection of the Historical Society of Pennsylvania." *Pennsylvania Magazine of History and Biography* 30 (1906): 376–78, 503.

   Letters to Humphreys relating to naval construction.

41. Smith, Philip C. F. *The Frigate Essex Papers: Building the Salem Frigate, 1798–1799.* Salem, Mass.: Peabody Museum of Salem, 1974. 334 pp.

Secondary Literature

42. Baker, Maury. "Cost Overrun, an Early Naval Precedent: Building the First U.S. Warships, 1794–98." *Maryland Historical Magazine* 72 (Fall 1977): 361–72.

43. Barrows, John S. "The Beginning and Launching of the United States Frigate *Constitution.*" *Proceedings of the Bostonian Society* (January 20, 1925): 22–37.

44. Bass, William P. "Who Did Design the First U.S. Frigates?" *Naval History* 5 (Summer 1991): 49–54.

45. Bauer, K. Jack. "Naval Shipbuilding Programs, 1794–1860." *Military Affairs* 29 (Spring 1965): 29–40.

46. Chapelle, Howard I. *The History of the American Sailing Navy: The Ships and Their Development.* New York: W. W. Norton, 1949. 558 pp.

47. Dunne, W. M. P. "The South Carolina Frigate: A History of the U.S. Ship *John Adams.*" *American Neptune* 47 (Winter 1987): 22–32.

48. Eddy, Richard. "'. . . Defended by an Adequate Power': Joshua Humphreys and the 74-Gun Ships of 1799." *American Neptune* 51 (Summer 1991): 173–94.

49. Emery, William M. *Colonel George Claghorn, Builder of Constitution.* Old Dartmouth Historical Sketches, No. 56. New Bedford, Mass.: Old Dartmouth Historical Society, January 1931. 12 pp.

50. Ferguson, Eugene S. "The Figure-head of the United States Frigate *Constellation.*" *American Neptune* 7 (October 1947): 255–60.

51. ———. "The Launch of the United States Frigate *Constellation.*" United States Naval Institute *Proceedings* 73 (September 1947): 1090–95.

52. Fisher, Charles R. "The Great Guns of the Navy, 1797–1843." *American Neptune* 36 (October 1976): 276–95.

53. ———. "Gun Drill in the Sailing Navy, 1797 to 1840." *American Neptune* 41 (April 1981): 85–92.

54. Fowler, William M., Jr. "America's Super-Frigates." *Mariner's Mirror* 59 (February 1973): 49–56.

55. Gilkerson, William. *Boarders Away: With Steel; The Edged Weapons and Polearms of the Classical Age of Fighting Sail, 1626–1826.* . . . Lincoln, R.I.: Andrew Mowbray, 1991. 160 pp.

56. ———. *Boarders Away II: With Fire; The Small Firearms and Combustibles of the Classical Age of Fighting Sail, 1626–1826.* . . . Lincoln, R.I.: Andrew Mowbray, 1993. 331 pp.

57. Gillmer, Thomas C. *Old Ironsides: The Rise, Decline, and Resurrection of the USS Constitution.* Camden, Maine: International Marine, 1993. 239 pp.

58. Gorr, Louis F. "The Foxall-Columbia Foundry: An Early Defense Contractor in Georgetown." In *Records of the Columbia Historical Society, 1971–72,* edited by Francis C. Rosenberger, 34–59. Washington: Columbia Historical Society, 1973.

59. Humphreys, Henry H. "Who Built the First United States Navy?" *Journal of American History* 10 (First Quarter 1916): 49–89.

   Joshua Humphreys's great grandson used documentary evidence to substantiate his great grandfather's place as the designer and constructor of the navy's first vessels.

60. Laing, Alexander. *American Ships.* New York: American Heritage Press, 1971. 536 pp.

61. Leiner, Frederick C. "The Subscription Warships of 1798." *American Neptune* 46 (Summer 1986): 141–58.

   History of the nine privately financed, privately constructed naval vessels.

62. Martin, Tyrone G., and John C. Roach. "Humphreys's Real Innovation." *Naval History* 8 (March/April 1994): 32–37.

   One of Joshua Humphreys's contributions to the design of three of the first frigates was a structural system of diagonal riders spanning a ship's lower hull to offset hogging.

63. Maurer, Maurer. "Coppered Bottoms for the United States Navy, 1794–1803." United States Naval Institute *Proceedings* 71 (June 1945): 692–99.

64. Perry, Percival. "The Naval-Stores Industry in the Old South, 1790–1860." *Journal of Southern History* 34 (November 1968): 509–26.

65. Pinkowski, Edward. "Joshua Humphreys." In *Forgotten Fathers*, 273–87. Philadelphia: Sunshine Press, 1953.

66. Rachal, William M. E. "When Virginia Owned a Shipyard: The Story of the Norfolk Naval Shipyard at Portsmouth to the Time of Its Purchase by the United States in 1801." *Virginia Cavalcade* 2 (Autumn 1952): 31–35.

67. Roosevelt, Franklin D. "Our First Frigates: Some Unpublished Facts about Their Construction." *Transactions of the Society of Naval Architects and Marine Engineers* 22 (1914): 139–53.

68. Stanton, Elizabeth B. "Builder of the First American Navy." *Journal of American History* 2 (First Quarter 1908): 101–12.

Correspondence of Josiah Fox attesting to his role in the construction of the first naval ships.

69. Todd, Thomas A. "USF *CONSTELLATION* as She May Have Appeared in the Period 1797 to 1800." *Nautical Research Journal* 31 (June 1985): 55–67.

70. Tucker, Spencer C. "Arming the Fleet: Early Cannon Founders to the United States Navy." *American Neptune* 45 (Winter 1985): 35–40.

71. ———. *Arming the Fleet: U.S. Navy Ordnance in the Muzzle-Loading Era*. Annapolis: Naval Institute Press, 1989. 308 pp.

72. Westlake, Merle T., Jr. "Josiah Fox, Gentleman, Quaker, Shipbuilder." *Pennsylvania Magazine of History and Biography* 88 (July 1964): 316–27.

Josiah Fox's major contributions to the design and construction of the first ships for the U.S. Navy.

73. Wood, Virginia Steele. *Live Oaking: Southern Timber for Tall Ships*. 1981. Reprint. Annapolis: Naval Institute Press, 1995. 206 pp.

Naval Operations

Documents

74. "American Naval Affairs, 1798–1802." *Bulletin of the New York Public Library* 11 (September 1907): 411–19.

   Benjamin Stoddert sends instructions to Commodore Richard Dale that authorize the capture of French armed vessels.

75. Truxtun, Thomas. *Instructions, Signals, and Explanations, Offered for the United States Fleet.* Baltimore: Printed by John Hayes, 1797. 38 pp.

76. ———. *Remarks, Instructions, and Examples Relating to the Latitude & Longitude; also the Variation of the Compass.* Philadelphia: Printed by T. Dobson, 1794. 31 pp.

   Includes appendices on masts and the general duties of officers of ships of war.

Secondary Literature

77. Emmons, George F., comp. *The Navy of the United States, from the Commencement, 1775–1853; with a Brief History of Each Vessel's Service and Fate as Appears upon Record.* Washington: Gideon & Co., 1853. 208 pp.

78. Harmon, Judd S. "Suppress and Protect: The United States Navy, the African Slave Trade, and Maritime Commerce, 1794–1862." Ph.D. diss., College of William and Mary, 1977. 282 pp.

79. Hollis, Ira N. *The Frigate Constitution: The Central Figure of the Navy under Sail.* Boston: Houghton Mifflin, 1931. 285 pp.

80. Martin, Tyrone G. *A Most Fortunate Ship: A Narrative History of "Old Ironsides."* Rev. ed. Chester, Conn.: Globe Pequot Press, 1982. 388 pp.

Relations with Barbary Powers

Documents

81. United States Office of Naval Records and Library. *Naval Documents Related to the United States Wars with the Barbary Powers: Naval Operations Including Diplomatic Background from 1785 through 1807.* Washington: Government Printing Office, 1939–44. 6 vols.

Secondary Literature

82. Allen, Gardner W. *Our Navy and the Barbary Corsairs.* 1905. Reprint. Hamden, Conn.: Archon Books, 1965. 354 pp.

83. Anderson, R. C. "Tripoli and Tunis: The Americans in the Mediterranean, 1795–1805." In *Naval Wars in the Levant, 1559–1853,* 393–426. Princeton: Princeton University Press, 1952.

84. Barnby, H. G. *The Prisoners of Algiers: An Account of the Forgotten American-Algerian War, 1785–1797.* London: Oxford University Press, 1966. 343 pp.

85. Bartlett, Harley H. "American Captivities in Barbary." *Michigan Alumnus Quarterly Review* 61 (Spring 1955): 238–54.

    Relates the captures of Americans by the Barbary powers and diplomatic efforts to end them.

86. Carr, James A. "John Adams and the Barbary Problem: The Myth and the Record." *American Neptune* 26 (October 1966): 231–57.

87. Chidsey, Donald B. *The Wars in Barbary: Arab Piracy and the Birth of the United States Navy.* New York: Crown, 1971. 165 pp.

88. Dudley, William S. "The Origins of the U.S. Navy's Mediterranean Squadron, 1783–1816." In *Français et Anglais en Méditerranée de la Révolution française à l'independance de la Grèce (1789–1830).* Journées franco-britanniques d'histoire de la Marine (3rd, 1990, Toulon, France). 251–60. [Vincennes, France]: Service historique de la Marine, 1992.

89. Field, James A., Jr. *America and the Mediterranean World, 1776–1882.* Princeton: Princeton University Press, 1969. 485 pp.

90. Folayan, Kola. *Tripoli during the Reign of Yūsuf Pāshā Qaramānlī.* Ile-Ife, Nigeria: University of Ife Press, 1979. 203 pp.

91. Gibbons, Patrick J. "Corsairs, Privateers, and Pirates: A Reconsideration of the Barbary Wars, c. 1780–1805." Master's thesis, University of Virginia, 1993. 101 pp.

92. Hunt, Livingston. "Bainbridge under the Turkish Flag." United States Naval Institute *Proceedings* 52 (June 1926): 1147–62.

Bainbridge's humiliating treatment at the hands of the Barbary powers.

93. Irwin, Ray W. *The Diplomatic Relations of the United States with the Barbary Powers, 1776–1816.* Chapel Hill: University of North Carolina Press, 1931. 225 pp.

94. Kitzen, Michael L. S. *Tripoli and the United States at War: A History of American Relations with the Barbary States, 1785–1805.* Jefferson, N.C.: McFarland, 1993. 203 pp.

95. Kortepeter, Carl M. "The United States Encounters the Middle East: The North African Emirates and the U.S. Navy (1783–1830)." *Revue d'Histoire Maghrebine* (Tunisia) 10 (December 1983): 301–13.

Traces the extensive official and private contacts, financial holdings, and private interests of the United States in the Middle East.

96. Tucker, Glenn. *Dawn Like Thunder: The Barbary Wars and the Birth of the U.S. Navy.* Indianapolis: Bobbs-Merrill, 1963. 487 pp.

97. United States Office of Naval Records and Library. *Register of Officer Personnel, United States Navy and Marine Corps and Ships' Data, 1801–1807.* Washington: Government Printing Office, 1945. 86 pp.

98. Van Alstyne, Richard W. "The Mediterranean Trade and the Barbary Powers." In *American Diplomacy in Action: A Series of Case Studies.* 2d ed. Stanford Books in World Politics. 497–503. Palo Alto: Stanford University Press, 1947.

99. Whipple, A. B. C. *To the Shores of Tripoli: The Birth of the U.S. Navy and Marines.* New York: William Morrow, 1991. 357 pp.

100. Wilson, Gary E. "The First American Hostages in Moslem Nations, 1784–1789." *American Neptune* 41 (July 1981): 208–23.

Quasi-War with France

Documents

101. "Extract from the Log of the Frigate *Boston.*" *Proceedings of the Massachusetts Historical Society* 20 (June 1883): 269–74.

   Engagement with French Navy corvette *Berceau.*

102. McKee, Christopher, ed. "*Constitution* in the Quasi-War with France: The Letters of John Roche, Jr., 1798–1801." *American Neptune* 27 (April 1967): 135–49.

   A midshipman's letters to his father reporting events while on *Constitution.*

103. Murray, William Vans. "Letters of William Vans Murray to John Quincy Adams, 1797–1803." Edited by Worthington Chauncey Ford. In *Annual Report of the American Historical Association for the Year 1912*, 341–708. Washington: Government Printing Office, 1914.

   Murray's diplomatic efforts to resolve differences with France.

104. United States Office of Naval Records and Library. *Naval Documents Related to the Quasi-War between the United States and France: Naval Operations from February 1797 to December 1801.* Washington: Government Printing Office, 1935–1938. 7 vols.

Secondary Literature

105. Allen, Gardner W. "The *Boston* and the *Berceau.*" *Proceedings of the Massachusetts Historical Society* 65 (October 1933): 163–68.

   History of the capture, detention, and return of the French navy corvette *Berceau.*

106. ———. *Our Naval War with France.* 1909. Reprint. Hamden, Conn.: Archon Books, 1967. 323 pp.

107. Anderson, William G. "John Adams, the Navy, and the Quasi-War with France." *American Neptune* 30 (April 1970): 117–32.

108. DeConde, Alexander. *The Quasi-War: The Politics and Diplomacy of the Undeclared War with France, 1797–1801.* New York: Scribner, 1966. 498 pp.

109. Dunn, Lucius C. "The Frigate *Constellation* Puts to Sea." United States Naval Institute *Proceedings* 74 (August 1948): 1004–7.

110. Dunne, W. M. P. "The *Constellation* and the *Hermione.*" *Mariner's Mirror* 70 (February 1984): 82–85.

   A mutineer from HMS *Hermione* enlisted in *Constellation* and incited mutinous talk in the U.S. frigate between June and August 1798 until he was discovered.

111. Hill, Peter P. *William Vans Murray, Federalist Diplomat: The Shaping of Peace with France, 1797–1801.* Syracuse, N.Y.: Syracuse University Press, 1971. 241 pp.

112. Kihn, Phyllis. "The French San Domingo Prisoners in Connecticut." *Connecticut Historical Society Bulletin* 28 (April 1963): 47–63.

   The capture of French schooner la *Vengeance* by U.S. sloop of war *Trumbull* and the subsequent holding of the prisoners from la *Vengeance* in Connecticut.

113. Knight, David C. *The Naval War with France, 1798–1800.* New York: Franklin Watts, 1970. 72 pp.

114. Kyte, George W., ed. "Guns for Charleston: A Case of Lend-Lease in 1798–1799." *Journal of Southern History* 14 (August 1948): 401–8.

The British loaned cannon and shot to America during the Quasi-War with France. Includes the correspondence of Robert Liston, Lord Grenville, and Timothy Pickering.

115. Leiner, Frederick C. "Anatomy of a Prize Case: Dollars, Side-Deals, and *Les Deux Anges.*" *American Journal of Legal History* 39 (April 1995): 1–19.

The frigate *Boston*'s capture of the prize les *Deux Anges* and the subsequent litigation, which went all the way to the United States Supreme Court, between Captains George Little and Silas Talbot.

116. ———. "The Baltimore Merchants' Warships: *Maryland* and *Patapsco* in the Quasi-War with France." *Maryland Historical Magazine* 88 (Fall 1993): 260–85.

117. Martin, Tyrone G. "Underway Replenishment, 1799–1800." *American Neptune* 46 (Summer 1986): 159–64.

How the *Constitution* maintained its station and replenished supplies.

118. Morgan, Mike. "The Remarkable Frigate L'*Insurgente.*" *Nautical Research Journal* 20 (April 1974): 134–37.

119. Palmer, Michael A. *Stoddert's War: Naval Operations During the Quasi-War with France, 1798–1801.* Columbia: University of South Carolina Press, 1987. 313 pp.

120. Russo, John Paul. "Hull's First Victory, One Painting: Three Famous Men." *American Neptune* 25 (January 1965): 29–34.

Lieutenant Isaac Hull captured French privateer *Sandwich* in May 1800.

121. Savageau, David LePere. "The United States Navy and Its 'Half War' Prisoners, 1798–1801." *American Neptune* 31 (July 1971): 159–76.

Treatment and disposition of captured French privateersmen.

122. Stansbury, David B. "The Quasi-War with France." *Naval History* 6 (Fall 1992): 16–21.

123. Stott, A. C. "Early Naval Strategy." United States Naval Institute *Proceedings* 62 (February 1936): 229–30.

Navigating abilities of Thomas Truxtun.

124. Van Alstyne, Richard W. "The Naval War with France, 1798–1800." In *American Diplomacy in Action: A Series of Case Studies.* 2d ed. Stanford Books in World Politics. 420–32. Palo Alto: Stanford University Press, 1947.

125. Votaw, Homer C. "The Sloop-of-War *Ganges.*" United States Naval Institute *Proceedings* 98 (July 1972): 82–84.

126. Welsh, Donald N. "The Quasi-War with France and the Creation of the United States Navy." Master's thesis, University of Akron, 1940. 81 pp.

127. Wood, Daniel N. "The All-Volunteer Force in 1798." United States Naval Institute *Proceedings* 105 (June 1979): 45–48.

Impressment and Relations with Great Britain

Documents

128. *Message from the President of the United States, Accompanying Sundry Papers Relative to the Impressment of American Seamen, from on Board Public Armed Vessels of the United States, by Vessels of War Belonging to the King of Great-Britain. . . . 8 January 1799.* Philadelphia: J. Gales, 1799. 8 pp.

129. Phillips, Isaac. *An Impartial Examination of the Case of Captain Isaac Phillips, Late of the Navy, and Commander of the United States Sloop of War Baltimore and Compiled from Original Documents and Records, with the Proceedings upon His Application to be Restored to His Rank in the United States Navy.* Baltimore: Benjamin Edes, 1825. 119 pp.

Secondary Literature

130. Campbell, John F. "The Havana Incident." *American Neptune* 22 (October 1962): 264–76.

   British impressment of fifty-five sailors from USS *Baltimore* on 16 November 1798.

131. Jackson, Scott Thomas. "Impressment and Anglo-American Discord, 1787–1818." Ph.D. diss., University of Michigan, 1976. 507 pp.

132. Palmer, Michael A. "Anglo-American Naval Cooperation, 1798–1801." *Naval History* 4 (Summer 1990): 14–20.

133. ———. "The Dismission of Capt. Isaac Phillips." *American Neptune* 45 (Spring 1985): 94–103.

   The captain of the USS *Baltimore* in 1798 who permitted his vessel to be boarded by a Royal Navy officer and fifty-five sailors to be pressed.

134. Perkins, Bradford. *The First Rapprochement: England and the United States, 1795–1805.* 1955. Reprint. Berkeley and Los Angeles: University of California Press, 1967. 257 pp.

135. Teignmouth, Henry N. S. "British Protection of American Shipping in the Mediterranean, 1784–1810." *United Service Magazine* n.s. 60 (December 1919): 169–78.

136. Zimmerman, James F. *Impressment of American Seamen.* 1925. Reprint. Port Washington, N.Y.: Kennikat Press, 1966. 279 pp.

The Officer Corps

General

137. Bradford, James C., ed. *Command under Sail: Makers of the American Naval Tradition, 1775–1850*. Annapolis: Naval Institute Press, 1985. 333 pp.

Studies of the naval officers who served in the navy during the Federalist period include William Bainbridge, John Barry, Stephen Decatur, Jr., Isaac Hull, Thomas Macdonough, Oliver Hazard Perry, Edward Preble, David Porter, and John Rodgers.

138. Cooper, James Fenimore. *Lives of Distinguished American Naval Officers*. 2 vols. in one. Philadelphia: Carey and Hart, 1846. 252 pp., 264 pp.

139. Guttridge, Leonard F., and Jay D. Smith. *The Commodores*. 1969. Reprint. Annapolis: Naval Institute Press, 1984. 340 pp.

Discusses the formative years of the U.S. Navy and its officers in the first six chapters.

140. McKee, Christopher. *A Gentlemanly and Honorable Profession: The Creation of the U.S. Naval Officer Corps, 1794–1815.* Annapolis: Naval Institute Press, 1991. 600 pp.

141. Pratt, Fletcher. *Preble's Boys: Commodore Preble and the Birth of American Sea Power.* New York: William Sloane, 1950. 419 pp.

    Contains short histories of the following officers whose careers began during the Federalist period: William Bainbridge, James Biddle, Johnston Blakeley, William Burrows, Stephen Cassin, Isaac Chauncey, Stephen Decatur, Jr., Isaac Hull, Jacob Jones, James Lawrence, Thomas Macdonough, Daniel Todd Patterson, David Porter, Charles Stewart, and Lewis Warrington.

Bainbridge, William

142. Dearborn, H. A. S. *The Life of William Bainbridge, Esq. of the United States Navy.* Princeton: Princeton University Press, 1931. 218 pp.

143. Long, David F. *Ready to Hazard: A Biography of Commodore William Bainbridge, 1774–1833.* Hanover, N.H.: University Press of New England, 1981. 359 pp.

Barron, James

144. Stevens, William Oliver. *An Affair of Honor: The Biography of Commodore James Barron, U.S.N.* Chesapeake, Va.: Norfolk County Historical Society, 1969. 204 pp.

145. Watson, Paul Barron. *The Tragic Career of Commodore James Barron, U.S. Navy (1769–1851).* New York: Coward-McCann, 1942. 84 pp.

Barry, John

146. Clark, William Bell. *Gallant John Barry, 1745–1803: The Story of a Naval Hero of Two Wars.* New York: Macmillan, 1938. 530 pp.

147. Griffin, Martin I. J. *Commodore John Barry, "The Father of the American Navy": The Record of His Services for Our Country.* Philadelphia: Published by the author, 1903. 424 pp.

148. Gurn, Joseph. *Commodore John Barry: Father of the American Navy.* New York: P. J. Kenedy & Sons, 1933. 318 pp.

Brown, Moses

149. Maclay, Edgar S. *Moses Brown, Captain, U.S.N.* New York: Baker & Taylor, 1904. 220 pp.

Dale, Richard

150. Hannon, Bryan. *Three American Commodores.* New York: Spinner Press, 1936. 208 pp.

Decatur, Stephen, Jr.

151. Anthony, Irvin. *Decatur.* New York and London: Scribner, 1931. 319 pp.

152. Lewis, Charles L. *The Romantic Decatur.* 1937. Reprint. Freeport, N.Y.: Books for Libraries Press, 1971. 296 pp.

153. Mackenzie, Alexander S. *Life of Stephen Decatur, a Commodore in the Navy of the United States.* Boston: Charles C. Little and James Brown, 1846. 443 pp.

Gordon, Charles

154. Calderhead, William L. "A Strange Career in a Young Navy: Captain Charles Gordon, 1778–1816." *Maryland Historical Magazine* 72 (Fall 1977): 373–86.

Hull, Isaac

155. Grant, Bruce. *Isaac Hull, Captain of Old Ironsides: The Life and Fighting Times of Isaac Hull and the U.S. Frigate Constitution.* Chicago: Pellegrini & Cudahy, 1947. 418 pp.

156. Hull, Isaac. *Commodore Hull: Papers of Isaac Hull, Commodore, United States Navy.* Edited by Gardner W. Allen. Boston: The Boston Athenaeum, 1929. 341 pp.

157. Maloney, Linda M. *The Captain from Connecticut: The Life and Naval Times of Isaac Hull.* Boston: Northeastern University Press, 1986. 549 pp.

158. Molloy, Leo T., comp. *Commodore Isaac Hull, U.S.N., His Life and Times.* Derby, Conn.: Hull Book Fund, 1964. 244 pp.

159. Richmond, Helen. *Isaac Hull: A Forgotten Hero.* Boston: USS *Constitution* Museum, 1983. 78 pp.

Lawrence, James

160. Burlington County Cultural and Heritage Commission (New Jersey). *The Captain James Lawrence Symposium Addresses.* Burlington, N.J.: Burlington County Cultural and Heritage Commission, 1983. 35 pp. Partial Contents: William M. Fowler, Jr., "The Navy of the New Republic, 1783–1815"; William S. Dudley, "Captain James Lawrence, USN: Fallen Naval Hero." Delivered on 3 October 1981 to commemorate the 200th anniversary of Lawrence's birth.

161. Gleaves, Albert. *James Lawrence, Captain, United States Navy, Commander of the "Chesapeake."* New York: Putnam, 1904. 337 pp.

162. Peabody Museum of Salem. *"Don't Give Up the Ship": A Catalogue of the Eugene H. Pool Collection of Captain James Lawrence.* Salem, Mass.: Peabody Museum, 1942. 82 pp.

Porter, David

163. Long, David F. *Nothing Too Daring: A Biography of Commodore David Porter, 1780–1843.* Annapolis: United States Naval Institute, 1970. 396 pp.

164. Porter, David D. *Memoir of Commodore David Porter of the United States Navy.* Albany, N.Y.: J. Munsell, 1875. 427 pp.

165. Turnbull, Archibald Douglas. *Commodore David Porter, 1780–1843.* New York and London: Century, 1929. 326 pp.

Preble, Edward

166. McKee, Christopher. *Edward Preble: A Naval Biography, 1761–1807.* Annapolis: Naval Institute Press, 1972. 394 pp.

Rodgers, John

167. Paullin, Charles O. *Commodore John Rodgers: Captain, Commodore, and Senior Officer of the American Navy, 1773–1838, a Biography.* 1910. Reprint. Annapolis: United States Naval Institute, 1967. 434 pp.

Talbot, Silas

168. Fowler, William M., Jr. *Silas Talbot: Captain of Old Ironsides.* Mystic, Conn.: Mystic Seaport, forthcoming 1995.

169. Tuckerman, Henry T. *The Life of Silas Talbot: A Commodore in the Navy of the United States.* New York: J. C. Riker, 1850. 137 pp.

Truxtun, Thomas

170. Eller, Ernest M. "Truxtun—the Builder." United States Naval Institute *Proceedings* 63 (October 1937): 1445–52.

Truxtun supervised the construction, rigging, and fitting out of *Constellation* and drew up the frigate's organization bills, orders, and regulations.

171. Ferguson, Eugene S. *Commodore Thomas Truxtun, 1755–1822: A Description of the Truxtun-Biddle Letters in the Collections of the Library Company of Philadelphia.* Philadelphia: Free Library of Philadelphia, 1947. 31 pp.

Letters written by Thomas Truxtun to Charles Biddle from 1 December 1787 to 21 October 1820.

172. ———. *Truxtun of the Constellation: The Life of Commodore Thomas Truxtun, U.S. Navy, 1755–1822.* 1956. Reprint. Annapolis: Naval Institute Press, 1982. 322 pp.

173. Robison, S. S. "Commodore Thomas Truxtun, U.S. Navy." United States Naval Institute *Proceedings* 58 (April 1932): 541–54.

Enlisted Personnel

174. Hoxse, John. *The Yankee Tar: An Authentic Narrative of the Voyages and Hardships of John Hoxse and the Cruises of the U.S. Frigate Constellation*. Northampton, Mass.: Printed by John Metcalf for the author, 1840. 200 pp.

175. Langley, Harold D. "The Negro in the Navy and Merchant Service, 1798–1860." *Journal of Negro History* 52 (October 1967): 273–86.

176. McKee, Christopher. "Fantasies of Mutiny and Murder: A Suggested Psycho-History of the Seaman in the United States Navy, 1798–1815." *Armed Forces and Society* 4 (Winter 1978): 293–304.

Uniforms

177. McBarron, H. Charles, and James C. Tily, "United States Navy, 1797 Full Dress." *Military Collector & Historian* 15 (Fall 1963): 80–81.

178. Magruder, John H., III. "U.S. Marine Corps, 1797–1804." *Military Collector & Historian* 8 (Spring 1956): 15–16.

179. Tily, James C. "Uniform for the Navy of the United States, 1797." *Military Collector & Historian* 15 (Winter 1963): 122–23.

180. ———. *The Uniforms of the United States Navy*. New York: T. Yoseloff, 1964. 338 pp.

Naval Discipline, Education, and Medicine

181. Burr, Henry L. *Education in the Early Navy.* Philadelphia: Published by the author, 1939. 228 pp.

This is the author's printed Ed.D. thesis from Temple University.

182. Langley, Harold D. "Edward Field: A Pioneer Practitioner of the Old Navy." *Connecticut Medicine* 46 (November 1982): 667–72.

183. ———. "Medical Men of the Old Navy: A Study in the Development of a Profession, 1797–1833." In *New Aspects of Naval History: Selected Papers from the 5th Naval History Symposium,* edited by the Department of History, United States Naval Academy, 69–79. Baltimore: Nautical and Aviation Publishing Co. of America, 1985.

184. ———. *Medicine in the Early U.S. Navy, 1794–1842.* Baltimore: Johns Hopkins University Press, 1995. 435 pp.

185. ———. *Social Reform in the United States Navy, 1798–1862.* Urbana: University of Illinois Press, 1967. 309 pp.

186. Paullin, Charles O. "Dueling in the Old Navy." United States Naval Institute *Proceedings* 35 (December 1909): 1155–97.

187. Pleadwell, Frank L. "Edward Cutbush, M.D.: The Nestor of the Medical Corps of the Navy." *Annals of Medical History* 5 (December 1923): 337–86.

188. Roddis, Louis H. "Naval Medicine in the Early Days of the Republic." *Journal of the History of Medicine and Allied Sciences* 16 (April 1961): 103–23.

189. Valle, James E. *Rocks & Shoals: Order and Discipline in the Old Navy 1800–1861*. Annapolis: Naval Institute Press, 1980. 341 pp.

Naval Art

190. Smith, Edgar Newbold. *American Naval Broadsides: A Collection of Early Naval Prints (1745–1815)*. Philadelphia: Philadelphia Maritime Museum, 1974. 225 pp.

191. Truxtun-Decatur Naval Museum, Washington, D.C. *Commodores Thomas Truxtun and Stephen Decatur and the Navy of Their Time: An Exhibition, Spring & Summer, 1950*. Washington: The Truxtun-Decatur Naval Museum, 1950. 39 pp.

192. United States National Archives. *The Old Navy, 1776–1860: A Catalog of an Exhibit of Prints and Watercolors from the Naval Collection of Franklin D. Roosevelt*. Washington: National Archives Trust Fund Board, General Services Administration, 1962. 56 pp.

Two prints in this work pertain to the Federalist period: one depicts the building of the frigate *Philadelphia* and the other is a view of *Constellation* capturing l'*Insurgente*.

193. United States Naval Academy, Annapolis. Museum. *American Naval Prints: from the Beverley R. Robinson Collection, U.S. Naval Academy Museum, Annapolis, Maryland.* [Washington]: International Exhibitions Foundation, 1976. 121 pp.

   The sole print applicable to the Federalist period is one of the American merchant ship *Planter* beating off a French privateer on 10 July 1799.

Marines

194. Dunn, Lucius C. "The *Constellation*'s First Marine Officer." *Maryland Historical Magazine* 43 (September 1948): 210–19.

   Lieutenant James Triplett and the first recruiting rendezvous for *Constellation.*

195. ———. "The U.S. Navy's First Seagoing Marine Officer." United States Naval Institute *Proceedings* 75 (August 1949): 918–23.

196. McClellan, Edwin N. "First Commandant of the Marine Corps, William Ward Burrows." *Daughters of the American Revolution Magazine* 59 (March 1925): 155–59.

197. ———. "From 1783–1798." *Marine Corps Gazette* 7 (September 1922): 273–86.

Establishment of the Marine Corps.

198. ———. "The Naval War with France." *Marine Corps Gazette* 7 (December 1922): 339–64.

199. Magruder, John H., III. "The Pig-tail Marines." *Marine Corps Gazette* 40 (February 1956): 46–7.

Marines and their queues.

Privateering

200. Bonnel, Ulane. "L'Apport Consulaire à la Reglementation de la Course et les Relations Franco-Américaine." ["Contributions of the Consulate to the Regulation of Privateers and Franco-American Relations."] *Revue de l'Institut Napoléon* 111 (1969): 159–67.

201. ———. *La France, les États-Unis et la Guerre de Course (1797–1815).* [*France, the United States and the War on Commerce (1797–1815)*]. Paris: Nouvelles Éditions Latines, 1961.

202. Jenkins, H. J. K. "Commerce Raiding and Crisis: Guadeloupe, 1799–1802." *American Neptune* 54 (Winter 1994): 18–24.

203. Knox, Dudley W. "Private Armed Ships Belonging to Salem, 1799." *Essex Institute Historical Collections* 71 (1935): 120–27.

204. Maclay, Edgar S. *A History of American Privateers*. New York: D. Appleton, 1899. 519 pp.

205. Pelzer, John D. "Armed Merchantmen and Privateers: Another Perspective on America's Quasi-War with France." *American Neptune* 50 (Fall 1990): 270–80.

   The defensive role of the American merchant marine in protecting American commerce.

206. Phillips, James D. "Salem's Part in the Naval War with France." *New England Quarterly* 16 (December 1943): 543–66.

Index of Authors

Note: Numerals refer to numbered items in the bibliography.

☆ U.S. GOVERNMENT PRINTING OFFICE: 1995   393–788